FROM EXILE TO FREEDOM
THE CHRONICLES OF MY LIFE

By Lizzie Toomer

*"Blessings"
Pastor Lizzie
Toomer*

Trilogy Christian Publishers
A Wholly Owned Subsidiary of Trinity Broadcasting Network
2442 Michelle Drive
Tustin, CA 92780

Copyright © 2021 by Lizzie Toomer

Unless otherwise noted, all scripture is taken from the New King James Version®. Copyright © 1982 by Thomas Nelson. Used by permission. All rights reserved.

The ESV® Bible (The Holy Bible, English Standard Version®). ESV® Text Edition: 2016. Copyright © 2001 by Crossway, a publishing ministry of Good News Publishers. The ESV® text has been reproduced in cooperation with and by permission of Good News Publishers. Unauthorized reproduction of this publication is prohibited. All rights reserved.

THE HOLY BIBLE, NEW INTERNATIONAL VERSION®, NIV® Copyright © 1973, 1978, 1984, 2011 by Biblica, Inc.® Used by permission. All rights reserved worldwide.

The Voice Bible Copyright © 2012 Thomas Nelson, Inc. The Voice™ translation © 2012 Ecclesia Bible Society All rights reserved.

All rights reserved, including the right to reproduce this book or portions thereof in any form whatsoever.
For information, address Trilogy Christian Publishing
Rights Department, 2442 Michelle Drive, Tustin, Ca 92780.

Trilogy Christian Publishing/ TBN and colophon are trademarks of Trinity Broadcasting Network.

For information about special discounts for bulk purchases, please contact Trilogy Christian Publishing.

Manufactured in the United States of America

Trilogy Disclaimer: The views and content expressed in this book are those of the author and may not necessarily reflect the views and doctrine of Trilogy Christian Publishing or the Trinity Broadcasting Network.

10 9 8 7 6 5 4 3 2 1

Library of Congress Cataloging-in-Publication Data is available.
ISBN 978-1-63769-414-5
ISBN 978-1-63769-415-2 (ebook)

Dedication

I dedicate this book to my children and grandchildren. In telling my story, I pray that you understand that our God is an awesome God.

I desire for you to learn that I did my best to let you how much I love you. I may have made mistakes, but they were never intentional. I love you all with an everlasting love from the deepest depths of my heart. I did not always know how to show it. I did not know who I was as a person. I looked for love in all the wrong places.

The day I let Jesus come into my life, everything changed for me. The purpose of this book, besides telling my story, is that I also want you to know that regardless of what you face in life, God is the answer.

Acknowledgements

I give thanks and praise to God for loving me unconditionally. Father, you have delivered me from all the tactics of the adversary to destroy my life, and for that I am eternally grateful.

To my overseers and apostles, Enos and Diane Chamberlain. I appreciate the prophetic word you released from God for me to write this book and for your attentiveness and patience with me. You encouraged me to grow in the faith by leaving nuggets of wisdom for me to learn from. You guy are the best spiritual parents a pastor could ask for.

To Nucleus Media, Stanley Nicole Dolly, and Reginald Brown. I thank you for your encouragement. Your compass directed me in the right direction to get my book started. Your advisement was epic for this project. I love you.

To my special daughter, Lola McGregor, who encourages and supports me in everything I do. Your father was right for telling me not to worry, for you do take good care of me. You are immeasurable. Your prayers were on point. I love and thank you.

To my baby daughter, Tiffany Jackson. Thank you for transcribing and conveying my story so lovely. Iron sharpens iron and we are sharper because of each other. I appreciate the hard work and long nights you put into this book. You are one of my beautiful heartbeats. Love you.

To Margret Wills. Words cannot say how timely you were with your support and prayers. I am thankful that you heard from God and was obedient to His will. Keep living life to its fullest.

Acknowledgements

To Darlisha Averitte. I know your mom is enormously proud of you and so am I. Thank you for your patience. You stepping up in the ministry took a ton of weight off of me. God allowed you to be a part of this project by you helping me to complete this book. I am forever grateful for you.

To my New Covenant Kingdom Ministries family, you have been tremendously supportive. Your calls, visits, prayers have uplifted me when I was in the valley. You have encouraged me while on the mountain top. I could not have asked for a more protective and loving congregation.

To my niece and nephew, Lanasia and Brandon Baldwin. Thank you for traveling to Indiana to get that perfect shot of me. I love you.

Thank you TBN team, Mark, Rachel, and Samantha for your guidance and help in editing and publishing my first book. May God bless you all richly.

Table of Contents

Silence of Exile and Existence	9
She Played It Safe	13
Play Pen	17
General Relief	21
I Lived How I Felt	25
Obviously	29
I Know This Sounds Crazy	37
But God Saved Me	41
Cues and Symbols	45
Reopened Wounds	53
The Call Of Life: Where Destiny Meet Purpose	57
Pitfalls: I Never Saw Them Coming	63
The Sum of It All	69

Introduction

I was born during an era of silence. I was held captive from the desires of my parental figures and guardians. I was exiled and banished from the beginning of a normal, healthy life of a little girl. I will chronicle as best as I can recall the experiences of my life as a result from their intensive flames and the effects of me living in the silence of exile and existence. I learned during the era held in captivity that it was unwise to speak out, especially as that of a young child. I did not realize until later in life that these were tactics of the adversary to hold me captive. To silence me. To cripple me into believing that I had no power and to tell me that I do not exist. I do not matter.

SILENCE OF EXILE AND EXISTENCE

I was inspired to tell my story for a few different reasons. The main reason was God told me to write down my life story. I struggled with reliving some of the situations I have been through. The second reason was that I desired to leave a legacy for my children and grandchildren. I was talking to my granddaughter, who asked question after question and I realized that no one truly knew my real-life story. Finally, I want my family and friend to see how great our God really is.

My name is Lizzie Toomer. My parents were Sylvester and Mary Lee Buckhanan. There were eight of us. Three boys and five girls. I am the only one who is still alive today.

I do not recall much about my early childhood. There are a few incidents I recall clearly. We, my siblings and I, often stayed with family members. My parent was married but they had an off-and-on type marriage. We mostly stayed with my grandma, which was my mother's mother, until she would return home. It was always a house full of people. A few of my unwed aunties and their offspring lived with Grandma Cora Lee.

We lived in Union Springs, Alabama. Grandma's house was big, at least that is how I recall it. I would spend many days at Grandma Cora Lee house. We all had daily chores to do. In those days, for a family to survive, the whole family had to lend a hand. There was no such thing as being too young to work. The house was always being cleaned. Someone had to cook. Someone had to go fetch water or wood. You helped in the garden tilling, planting seed, and pulling weeds. Then when harvest came, you harvested the food you had grown. I recall sitting on that porch picking greens and snapping peas and green beans. Whatever we grew in the garden had to be prepped for eating or storing it for later use.

It was in the country. There were no streets. Just dirt roads. No streetlights or signs to navigate your destination. No one had gas stoves. The heating and cooking had to be done by firewood. The was no running water in the house. We had a well with a pump handle to pump water into a bucket to take inside the house. It had an outhouse that sat out back.

As hard as I worked, I also played hard. My siblings and cousins would run in the yard playing tag or the game called "You Are It." We made up games to entertain ourselves. We would play for hours after our homework and chores were done.

I was happy but naïve. Illiterate to the woes of life. I come from the generation that says children are to be seen but not heard. You as a child did not have an opinion. Well, we did but it was not solicited. You were to be quiet and mind your manners. Do as you are told. So, I did not ask a lot of questions about my home environment. I believed that my life was normal. Well, not until that dreadful night.

My father was not a thug, but he loved the actions and tensions of gambling. I was told that his gambling was to validate the risk taking to define his manhood. There was no need for such a risk in my opinion, for we all loved my father.

My father had this compulsiveness and persistent habit of betting on card games and rolling dice. My father was killed at a gambler's game. He substituted betting on his card games and rolling dice over the real value of his children and wife.

I was about six years old at the time when I leaned of the news from my Aunt Cora. My siblings and I were fast asleep, when my Aunt Cora, my mother's sister, came into the room.

She said, "Lizzie, you all wake up. You all daddy is dead!"

I got up, but was somewhat confused, not truly comprehending what had just transpired. I would have never guessed that my life was about to change drastically. I do not remember how my siblings responded to this news. I recall just feeling numb. Our father that we loved dearly was gone.

Daddy was kind to us. He would visit us often at Grandma Cora Lee's house. He would bring us presents and candy, along with kisses and hugs. Despite whatever my parents had going on between the two of them, they kept us out of their situation. They showed us love the best way they knew how.

I learned later in life that my father was murdered over a five-dollar bet. What was so valuable to me and my family was snuffed out over such a small amount of money—just a man trying to make more money for his family. The man that shot my father was a sore loser. He had lost and claimed that my father was cheating. He proclaimed that he was going to get his gun and if my father was still there when he came back, he was going to kill him. I was informed that the murderer had lost his mule to my father the year prior. Back then, you needed a mule to help you till the ground. No mule made it harder to work your fields. My uncle on my father's side of the family had stated that he would give the man five dollars for his loss. He refused it from my uncle. He was angry and wanted my father to be the one who paid him.

I wished my father had left the game once the man that had threatened him left to get his gun. That is the chance you take when you participate in a gambler's game.

SHE PLAYED IT SAFE

My mother came back into town from wherever she had been enjoying her mere pleasures. I recall a funeral. Everyone around me was sad. I just remained numb to the whole situation. There were discussions on what was to occur next. My mother needed to obtain work to provide for us. This was at the end of spring. She had decided to take my siblings with her because they were able to work. My family was what they call pickers. They would go from farm to farm to harvest the crops. I was to be left with my father's sister Eland and her husband. It was explained to me that if I went with them, someone would have to babysit me. This meant that it would be one less person to bring in income.

My mother left me. She played it safe by leaving me at the doorsteps of my aunt.

"You sit right there and don't you move," she said.

Only a few days after my father's funeral, my whole family packed up to go to Florida to work. That day they drove off was the second saddest day of my life.

I am speaking from my memory and my personal space. More clearly by, my permissive will. For me, there is nothing more damaging than a parent who never valued me. I felt as if it was not a pain for my mother to lose me. I felt that she never truly saw me. In fact, she saw right past me. My mother never connected with me inside my personal wellbeing. She detached from me after my father had been killed and once again after his funeral. My new reality was this: days after my father's funeral, my mother and siblings would move. I was left with my aunt and uncle to raise me, a deliberate choice that my mom made. That final decision to leave me with my dad's sister and not to protect nor comfort me by taking me with her crushed my spirit. My father did not stay. My mother did not stay. I was permitted to stay and remain all alone by deliberate will.

My aunt's house was big like Grandma Cora Lee's house. The

house sat on cement blocks. It held the house high off the ground. High enough that a small child could walk up under it.. The porch ran the whole length of the house. It had approximately six to eight steps going up to the porch. I sat on the bottom step.

My mother promised to come back and get me in the fall. Mom and my siblings all loaded up in the car. It was a black Ford. They turned to wave goodbye to me. I waved back. I was wearing a white sundress with lime green and orange flowers. It was my favorite dress that my mother had brought for me. I sat there long after they had left. I want them to turn the car around and say, "Come on Lizzie and get in the car with us." But that did not happen. I wanted to cry. I am not sure why the tears never flowed. I just sat there and allowed my heart to break. This was another lesson that I would face over the chronicles of my life. The lesson of how a parent or a person at will deliberately avoids you. The pain felt like someone took a knife and stuck it through my heart. It would take years of being in pain before I receive my healing and deliverance.

I can still here my aunt's voice. She came to the front door and said, "There is no need to cry and mope around. Get up from there and go get some wood for the stove." I did not correct her by telling her I was not crying. I did as I was told. My uncle was nice and would often protect me from my strict aunt. They were good to me. I wanted for nothing. Aunty was strict because of the things she had experienced in her life. It caused her anxiety and mistrust of others that was not her family or friend. She wanted to keep me safe from life's misfortunes.

My aunt and uncle had little education. I think my aunt only had a second-grade education. In the days that she was being raised, the kids were needed to help work the land or help in the house. Education was secondary to providing life's essentials.

My uncle was offered an opportunity to come up north with his brother, who already lived in Indiana. The factories up north were

She Played it Safe

doing massive hiring in the 1950s. He was offered a job with General Motors. That was a few months after my father's death and my family moved to Florida. This was at the end of the summer. Harvest time was not over yet. My aunt and uncle packed us up and moved to Indiana before my mother could return to Union Springs to get me.

I was angry because my mother left me. I did not understand why me out of all my siblings. That question would be on my mind for years to come. Why me? I do not know, maybe she left me due to the varying hardships of economic frustrations or tensions buried among her misery. She played it safe.

There is something very odd about a mother abandoning a child of her own body. One reason my mom made this choice might have been her own unhappiness and misery while fighting for her own survival. Nothing really remained for an individual like my mother to cling to for getting along in this world.

In the years that followed, I was no longer held captive in exile and silence. I would remind my mother of my story and as a casualty of many injuries and compromises, I became a resentful and undermined little girl to a woman. Later in life, I too experienced and expressed her point of view by playing it safe.

PLAY PEN

It has been approximately ten years since the move to Indiana. I am now sixteen years old. My mother and I have not laid eyes on each other in all that time. I recalled a conversation between my mother and my aunt after we moved to Indiana. My aunt was telling my mother to send for me to come back to Alabama. My mother explained to my aunt that she did not ask for me to be sent to Indiana but that she entrusted me to their care in Alabama. She was adamant about them sending me back to the place where she had left me. They were arguing over who was going to pay for my return to my mother. This is needless to say, but I remained in Indiana.

I kept in touch with one of my sisters. She is the one that explained to me that I was too young to go work in Florida with the rest of my family. I never really understood that explanation. I have a brother that is a year younger than me, and yet he was able to go with the rest of my family. My sister lived with my aunt and uncle during the time our father were slanged but choose to leave with our mother to help her provide for the family.

The spring I turned sixteen, my sister, who now stayed in Cleveland, Ohio, had shared with me that our mother was coming to visit her in the summer. She offered for me to come visit her at the same time Mom was to come. I agreed, for I was excited to see my mother once again. It had been an awfully long time coming. The plan was I was going to tell my guardians that I was just going to visit but my mother, sister, and older brother had planned on me staying with them.

I got to Cleveland before my mother arrived. We waited all day the day before for her bus to come. It was running extremely late and it did not get there until the wee hours of the next morning. We were all still asleep when she reached my sister's home. Someone yelled, "Lizzie, wake up, your mother is here!" At the sight of my mother, I thought that she was beautiful. Milk chocolate skin with a

Coca-Cola-shaded body. She had a look of sadness and anger on her face. Sad from all the hardships she had endured in life. I believe the angry look was a form of protection to warn anyone off that would dare to take advantage of her again. Complications in life had sucked the joy from her. I broke down and began to sob out of control. My emotions were exceedingly high. She came and gave me a big hug. I noticed that she did not seem to be as excited to see me as I was to see her.

Have you ever wanted something extremely bad and dreamed of how awesome it was going to be when you finally obtained that very thing, dream, or idea? In reality, it goes nothing like you have fantasized about. I do not know what all transpired in my mother's life over the past ten years. I can say this as a matter of fact: it stole parts of her and held it for ransom, ransom that she was unable to pay for she had already paid too high of a price.

We were all supposed to be one happy family now that some of us were back together. My older brother was going to get a house big enough for us to stay in. I was excited to be back with my family. I was not going anywhere. We were finally going to be a family again. Well, that was short-lived. By the end of the summer, my brother and mother had gotten into a huge argument. I had seen sides of my family that I did not care for. The manner in which they spoke to one another was atrocious.

Growing up under my aunts and uncle roof, I never had experienced people talking or treating someone they love in that manner. Yes, my aunt was strict, but she always taught me a level of respect for family. She drove the importance of having morals and respect for your family. It was about supporting and helping a loved one whenever you can. You do not say things that will cause harm to someone else. Seeing this displayed right before my eyes was a rude awakening for me. In time, I would receive a lot of eye-opening experiences about my family.

After my mother and brother's argument, my mother decided to move back to Florida. She wanted me to come with her to Florida. Wow, my mother wanted me to be with her in Florida. This may be my opportunity to cultivate that relationship with her that I so desired. We set off for the palm trees and ocean. I was excited to be leaving Cleveland with my mom. I did not tell my guardians that I was not planning on coming back home to Anderson ever.

When we got to Florida, my mother enrolled me into school. As we started living our day-to-day life with each other along with my one of my sisters and her kids, I noticed that life had taken a toll on my mother. This woman was nothing like I had dreamed her to be. She was a bitter and angry woman. I felt that my mom had some type of notion toward me and my up bringing. I believe she thought that I was spoiled.

At my mom's house, I was expected to pull my weight at sixteen. Going to school was fine, as long as I could pay my share of rent, groceries, and whatever expenditures there were.

In Florida, we lived next door to an older Pentecostal couple. They would sometimes take my nieces and I to evening church services. On one of those nights, I had an encounter with the Lord. I am not sure why I had that encounter with Him because I was not seeking for Him or praying, but He was thinking about me.

"Who has saved us and called us with a holy calling, not according to our works, but according to His own purpose and grace which was given to us in Christ Jesus before the ages began" (2 Tim. 1:9).

The power of the Holy Spirit overwhelmed me. The members of the church were singing songs of praise. I stared singing and dancing uncontrollably. Tears ran down my face. I could not stop giving God praise even when everyone else had stopped. It was to the point whereas I was rolling on the ground.

I heard the preacher say, "We haven't had a person get saved like that in a long time. We need to baptize her as soon as possible."

When I finally got up from the floor, I was greatly embarrassed because I could not control myself in front of my nieces. The very next day the preacher did baptize me.

By now I was not feeling my new environment living with my mother. I was ready to go back to that life I now know was not as bad as I thought. I did not know about the story of the prodigal son currently at this time, but I felt just like he did when he compared his new lifestyle with his old lifestyle. I remembered how well I had it in Indiana, and I needed to return there. At home in Indiana, I had been protected with no worries or cares about what I would eat, sleep, or wear. All I was responsible for was to do well in school and not get into trouble. I was trained to stay in the play pen. I had every toy I needed or wanted as long as I did not get out of the play pen. All I wanted was out of the play pen to roam around freely. When I got out of the play pen, I quickly realized that I was not able to walk. I wanted to go home and crawl back into the play pen. I needed for someone to think, talk, and walk for me. I called my aunt and uncle and asked if I could come home and would they send for me. They sent me a bus ticket and I left Florida. I was very relieved to be heading back to the play pen.

GENERAL RELIEF

I had been back in Anderson for a few months. It was fall and I did not attend school that semester. When I had gotten back home, school was already in session. I would have been so far behind in trying to catch up my schoolwork. My plan was to sit out until the next semester.

I was enjoying being back home. I was given a little more leniency in being able to hang out with my friends. I would go to the dances they would host by the high school or social clubs. Most Friday nights there would be a Sock Hop. We'd dance until our bodies were tired. There were only a small number of boys that could or would dance with the girls. We would take turns dancing with them. If there was not another boy available to dance with, we would dance with each other. There was this one boy that had caught my attention. We hung out a few times, but I soon found out that I was not the only one he was interested in spending time with. That was disheartening to witness. By now it was a little too late to undo what was done. I did not know what I was going to do about my new situation.

Mom had learned that all my siblings had gotten Social Security checks for the death of our father except for me. She applied for me to get a monthly check. I received a call from my mother telling me that I had to come back to Florida. She stated that I could be arrested for not being in school. I was seventeen at the time. She needed for me to be in Florida in order for her to get the Social Security benefits. I did not argue with her. I would return to Florida. Besides, I just found out that I was pregnant. I did not want anyone to know my secret.

Mom had accepted the life that she had been dealt to her. For her to survive with little to no education in this world, she had to do things the best way she knew how. Work wherever she could. Live wherever she could. She did whatever she could to make money to survive. I had no ill feelings about Mom wanting to get a check for me. I just desired to get to know her better.

Mom sent me a ticket. I was now back in Florida. I was trying to run away from my guardians being disappointment in me being unwed and pregnant. We both had a reason for me being there. Hers was the money. Mine was the shame.

I soon met another one of my older sisters that I had not seen since the day they left me in Alabama. She lived approximately fifty miles from our mother in a town called Lake Wales, Florida.

She had been observing me since she came to visit; observing how me and our mother was getting along and how Mom was concerned about acquiring that SSI check. One day, she asked me if I had seen a doctor since I found out I was pregnant. I told her no. She asked Mom if she could take me back with her. Her reasoning was so I could be checked out by a doctor. Mom allowed me to go, but firmly stated that I could only be gone a short while. I needed to be in her custody in order to get paid.

I knew when I left with my sister, that I was not returning to Clewiston. I had had my fill of this lifestyle. My mother and I were not developing the type of relationship I desired to have. I did not know then what I know now. Mom was not capable to love in the capacity I yearned for. Hurting people often hurt others. I do not believe it was intentional, but because she never knew love unconditionally. Years later, I would learn about her upbring. The hardships of her life. The things she endured to survive in this cold and calculating world.

Once I got to Lake Wales, I was seen by a doctor. I learned that Sissy did not have a good relationship with Mom either. I am not sure what their issue was with each other. I did not feel so bad knowing that a few of my siblings did not have a good connection with our mother. I had thought the reason Mom and I did not mesh well was because I was not raised by her, not understanding the fact that Mom had lack of experience of good relationships. From her childhood to adulthood. I guess it is like trying to be a basketball star without ever seeing someone play the game. No examples of a good relationship ever being displayed before her.

My sister worked with a group of people that she also party with. They would work hard all week and party on the weekends. My sister would sometimes host a party. I would be excited to attend these get togethers. I like the socializing with different types of people. She had a neighbor named Travis that I would find myself talking to at these get togethers. I thought that he was interesting. We started hanging out more often outside the parties. I started to really like being around him.

A few more months had gone by. I was due to have my baby. Travis knew that I was pregnant when we first started to get to know each other. I realized why Mom and sis did not get along well was because they were similar. She too had plans for my SSI check. With in the first few weeks of me being in Lake Wales, I went down to the Social Security Administration to change the address to where they would send my check. I gave them my address in Indiana. I had plans of my own. I was going to have my baby and soon after return to Indiana. When I got there, my check would be waiting on me. My aunt did not have an agenda about the money. She would keep the check until I returned home to claim it. It was not about the money for her. She just wanted me. When my baby was born, I did exactly what I planned. I returned home with my son and claimed the check.

I learned a lot about myself while in Florida. I understood that I was naïve and was not built for that fast life. The hustling lifestyle, doing whatever you had to in order to get one step ahead. I could not grasp that concept of "dog eat dog." My vibe was that of a small town where everybody looked out for each other.

A general relief occurred one day during a phone conversation with my mother. My mother acknowledged what happened and why I had taken on my identity crisis. Parts of my identity had been formed and shaped by the influences upon my physical, mental, emotional, and social make-up that were no longer difficult to define. My marriage was ending in a divorce and abandoment, which was regulated by avoidance of my issues. Migrating parent and guardian figures unerringly finding their way north and south, driven by influences to escape economic hardships, frustrations, and tensions of the changing seasons. I became fearful as a child from the abandonment. Relocating from my birthplace did not help. It was not a joyful experience.

These images and sensations of rejection and abandonment became my inheritance that influenced an important part of my thinking, as my mother explained herself that day. Her words became a general relief. It was a gift from her to me. I was thirty-four when I learned of this.

I LIVED HOW I FELT

After being back home, Travis and I continued to communicate with each other. He desired to really court me. He wanted to come to Indiana to be with me. I thought that I was in love with Travis. Even though Travis was not my son's father, I yearned for what they call a "normal" family. I wanted to have a family that consisted of a husband, wife, and child.

Travis made his way to Anderson. He met my aunt and uncle. Aunty thought that he was okay for me. In those days, if a man worked and took care of his family, that was a major accomplishment. There was little thought about his character or morals. If he was a provider, that is what mattered.

I married Travis. We had five children. My aunt would not let my first born live with us. She did not feel like my baby would be safe with Travis. She said that Travis was not his biological father and would not treat my son well. Aunty's concerns were not unwarranted. Some telltale signs had already occurred. Looking back, it is funny that she was okay with him marrying me, but not with him raising my son. I should have known then that something was not quite right about that situation.

There was not a happily ever after to this story. I was more miserable than I have ever been before in my life. I kept wondering if this was my fate to be shamed, hurting, and sad. He was a very controlling man, paranoid about everything and everybody that was around us. Travis was physically, verbally, and emotionally abusive to me and our kids. I could not listen to music, dance, smile, or be happy around this man without it causing some sort of paranoid, violent response. I would have to sneak to listen to music. I would only talk on the phone to friends when he was not at home. No one was allowed over because he suspected them of any and everything. I took the brunt of his abuse so that my children would not feel the wrath of his anger. Travis had issues with his childhood. It turned him into a terribly angry man. I became so afraid of him. I never knew what or when something would set him off. He liked me being afraid of him. It was specially designed that way for him to control me in that manner. The more Travis controlled me, the better he felt about himself.

I lived in that firestorm with my babies for nine long, torturous years. My fifth child as an adult child recalled how it was living with his father.

He said, "During the day we would be playing, laughing, and having fun until a certain time of the day. Mom would get this look on her face. The atmosphere would change from light and happiness to one of heaviness and fear. All the fun stop because it was time for him, Travis, to come home from work."

It pains me to know that memory is etched in my son's heart. I tried my best to protect them from all the craziness of our lives in those days.

I may have felt like I was unworthy of unconditional love but for my babies to experience this agony was unacceptable for me. It was affecting my children and that I could not live with. I never wanted them to endure all the heartache I experienced in my childhood. How I was living at this point in my life took me back to when my mother left me sitting on the steps. I felt as if no one ever loved me. No one ever fought for me. No one ever helped me without a personal agenda. I felt trapped in this cycle of defeat. I was stuck with no way out.

I thought, if this man would die, I could finally be free of this traumatic lifestyle. I would daydream about how lovely it would be to be at liberty to do as I please. I would live in a little house with my babies. Buy what I wanted. Go wherever I desired. Listen to music. Watch what I wanted on TV. One thing this man could not steal from me were my dreams of freedom. I recall a song in those days that said something to the fact of not losing your dreams because dreams can come true.

I Lived How I Felt

By now I was tired of living this torturous lifestyle. We had to get out of this whirlwind before it destroyed us all. I started to put a plan in motion for our exodus. I was working for General Motors and I began to set money aside for the day when I would walk out that door. I also found an apartment that I could move into once I was out of Travis's clutches.

Travis started to suspect something was going on with me. He would tell me I could never leave him and take our kids with me. I was threatened by him that if I tried to leave, he would take the kids. He implied that I would never see them again. This was low even for him because he knew my story of being left on the steps and how traumatic it was for me to grow up without my parents. He became tighter reigned with me. Travis sent for his mother to come to Indiana. I believe she was there to watch my every move while her son was gone. She was to report any questionable activities.

I got myself a lawyer. I informed him of my intentions on departing ways with Travis. I expressed my concerns for Travis stealing my kids. He said, "Lizzie if you get the chance to run, do so. That means if you must leave the kids to get free, do so. We can get your children back in your custody through the courts."

Soon after that conversation, I left the first chance I got. Of course, Travis left town with my babies except for our first son together. He and his mother packed up my children and whisked them away. He left while I was at work. I found this out the very next day when my attorney and law enforcement went to retrieve my kids.

I was devastated. I do not know how I was functioning. I would wake up in the middle of the night crying. I could imagine my kids calling out for me, "Momma, where are you? Momma, help me!" I did not know how my kids were being treated. I stated that he was a very abusive man and controlling. I was frightened that he was going to punish my kids for me leaving him.

This whole situation was overwhelming to me. I was not eating nor sleeping. My physician prescribed me some strong nerve pills. I was laid off work temporarily about a week after the kidnapping. I welcome the time off. I could not keep up with the expectations of me performing my job well.

Once again, I went numb. I put forth my best effort not to lose my faculties. My family and friends tried their hardest to comfort me. It was to no avail. Not because they were inadequate but because you cannot fill this type of void in a person's life. It was a destitute mindset to have.

I lived how I felt at that time by distortions and impairments so grave by allowing my aunt and husband to control me. I did not know how to think on my own. The most frightening idea is having no hope. This is not a fairy tale. I lived how I felt at that time.

Living by how I felt brought the experiences of no great emotional relief. Living by how I felt only surfaced guilt and self-punishment that would trespass upon me later.

I was not making good decisions on my own. After all, my mother had abandoned me and left me with haunting suspicions that I was an orphan, the imprint that my parents were unlinked to me. I needed and allowed someone to think for me, to tell me what I should do. I lived how I felt.

OBVIOUSLY

Now that I had left, and I was out of the clutches of my husband, I began to wonder where my kids were. Were they dead? Fear infiltrated my very being and thoughts. I was in a state of depression.

Travis had taken my second, my fourth, my fifth, and my sixth child. As I stated before, my firstborn was now living with my aunt and uncle. My third child had gone over to my aunt's to spend the night with his brother. So, Travis was not able to take all our kids. But knowing that did not ease my mind. I often cried wondering where they were and if they were all right.

During this season, I was introduced to a man through a friend. He was from Muncie but now lived in Anderson. He worked at the same factory that my friend worked at. He was kind of tall. Medium-brown complexion. He was exceptionally smooth with words and somewhat of a romantic. He was his mother's only child. She spoiled him, as some would say, rotten.

As I shared my story with him, he became concerned about my kids. Jackson had three kids of his own with his ex-wife in Muncie. I later learned that he genuinely loved kids. Years later, he developed a program in the city of Anderson for at-risk youth.

I like the way he consoled me. We started to develop a friendship/relationship. By now, my kids had been gone for a few months. It was nice to have a friend that was as much concerned about my children. I could share openly about the loss I was experiencing.

The days and months started flying by. Most of it was a blur. I spent most of my time over at my aunt and uncle's house. I would go over during the day so I could see the two children that were still in my presence. My family kept my third child the whole time while my other kids were missing.

It is now going on five or six months since Travis had snatched my kids and ran off with them. I worried about my kids nonstop. Where are they and why they have not been found? Are they okay?

Are they scared? I was at my wit's end. I need a breakthrough. I need answers. I need my kids. Lord, I need your help!

My attorney would check in on me from time to time. This day he called me and said, "Lizzie, we have found your children. They are in Bartow, Florida. Their paternal grandmother had been arrested, for the kids were found in her possession. We do not know where Travis is." For a moment, I was dazed. My heart was pounding hard against my chest. My breathing became frantic. And right before I could pass out, I heard the voice on the other end say, "But you have to go get them." That caused another wave of panic to go through me. For what seemed like hours but was only mere seconds, I stopped breathing. How was I going to get my babies?

Later that afternoon, I told my boyfriend about that phone call. I let him know that they had found my kids, but I had to go get them. With no hesitation Jackson said, "If we can get gas money, I will take you to go get them." I was not working at this time for my job had laid me off. I had not worked since the end of April.

I called my aunt and a few of my friends. I even asked a church or two for a donation. Soon the fives, tens, and twenties started to add up. We collected approximately $300. This was in 1972 and that was enough money for us to get there and back home on. We left the very next day which was a Wednesday.

Jackson drove a 1966 Bonneville Pontiac. We left Anderson early that morning and did not arrive in Bartow until late that night. We had been instructed by my attorney upon arrival to go to the Bartow Police Station. There, they would release my children to us. Remember that this was in the 1970s and we were now in the Deep South. There were parts of Florida where they still practiced segregation laws even though it was outlawed. There was a stench left from the dislike of ones with darker colored skin.

It did not go as we suspected. The whole experience was overwhelmingly crazy. The Bartow police took us through a grueling interrogation before they would devolve any information about my babies whereabouts. By now it is way past midnight. After the interrogation, we were informed that the officer with the information to where my kids were was not on duty and would not be in until after 9:00 a.m. We inquired about a motel that we could stay in. The place that was suggested was miles away and we were getting low on funds. It was only a few more hours before 9:00 a.m. We thought we would just stay in the car until then. The department proceeded to tell us that if we stayed in the parking lot to be careful because no one knew who we were and why we would be sitting in the Bartow police parking lot. We prayed that no one would say anything about us setting in the parking lot. Harassment from police towards African Americans in those days was extremely frightening and often life-threatening.

    With that information, Jackson and I took turns watching out for anything that may bring harm to us. One would sleep while the other would watch. Thank God nothing happened to us. We decided early that morning to drive to a gas station to freshen up, after which we drove right back to the police station. Upon our arrival once again, they took us through another interrogation. After what seems like hours, we were given the information to where my children were. They were in another city which was only about an hour away from Bartow.

    We had finally gotten the release papers for the foster mother to give them to us. As we were driving there, my emotions were well off the charts. An array of feelings came cross me. I was frightened, furious, sad, zealous, happy, and many additional adjectives during that ride.

    When I got there and knocked on the foster mother's door. I explained who I was and that I had the release paper for my children. She let us in her house. My heart was racing. At first sight of my babies, they looked so lost and forgotten. My two youngest ones did not recognize me.

I asked, "Do you know who I am?"

My fifth child asked, "Geraldine?"

Geraldine was a character that Flip Wilson played in his weekly variety series, *The Flip Wilson Show*. I broke down crying and I said, "No, I am your mother." By now we were all crying. I did not believe that I would ever see my kids again. I did not know if they would see me.

Thoughts of my mother leaving and me with the promise that she would come back for me that fall. It was years before I would see her again. I was so scared that history would repeat itself and I would not be able to see my seed again. I thank God that was not our destiny.

We said our goodbyes and thank you to the nice lady. We packed the kids in the car and started to head back to Indiana. Relieved to have my dear loves back in my presence, that scared and longing feeling for my seed was replaced with appreciation and admiration.

That feeling of euphoria was shortly lived. Not long after we had left the foster mother's home, we started running into car trouble. We stop to have the car serviced and we were told that we needed an alternator on the car. It was fixed and again we were on our way home. It did not take long before the car started acting funny again. We would only travel about thirty to forty miles down the road before the car would act as if it did not want to run.

We were now in Georgia, still part of the South where there was little tolerance for people of color. A police officer had stop to see why we were pulled over to the side of the road. He asked a few questions before offering Jackson a ride to the nearest gas station/garage auto repair shop. Back then they were one and the same. We were grateful but still scared. I was still scared to be left alone on the side of God only knows where with my incredibly young kids. It was about 1:00 or 2:00 in the morning.

There were a car approaching our vehicle. My nerves were on full alert. It turned out to be a woman with Jackson in the car. She was the girlfriend of the old black man from the garage. They jumped the car off so that we were able to get to the garage where the car would be repaired. We had little money left from spending on gas, food, and auto repairs. I could not imagine what we were going to do.

I started to ponder, since this was our third time stopping with car trouble, whether I should have left my kids in Florida. I believed that we were not going to make it home. Once again, my mindset was so confusing. I did not know how to think positive or to have good thoughts. I only thought negatively because I only experienced negative things. Let me explain why I thought like this. As we were leaving the Bartow Police Station, we were informed that the kids' paternal grandma was there in a cell. I felt that she was upset by the arrest. Their grandmother would practice all kinds of strange rituals and spells. She was a very superstitious woman. She often scared me when I was around her. It was this peculiar aura around her. I thought that maybe she had put some sort of curse on us.

Before I could suggest to my boyfriend that we should go back, the nice older man came and said that the car is fixed, and we can go. By now it is around 3:00 a.m. He discovered that the mechanic before him had put the wrong alternator on the Pontiac.

Once again, we said thank you and goodbye. We had hardly any money left after the repairs. We lived off crackers and soda pops until we made to Indianapolis, Indiana. Starving we stopped at White Castle to eat. We had $6.00 dollars to our names. White Castle burgers were only twelve cents at that time. We pigged out for we knew we only had a few miles, about twenty-five minutes, before we would be home. It was Friday and Jackson knew that he had a check waiting from his job.

Now being back home with all my kids. I was relieved to be back in my own place with the blessings God had given me. I was only home a week before I was called back to GM to start work again. I felt secure for a while knowing I was able to take care of my kids.

We settled into our house. Exhausted from the whole ordeal, I enrolled my kids that were old enough to go to school. I got a babysitter for the ones that were not old enough. I felt relieved and secure for the first time in a long time. That feeling was short-lived. I soon found out that I was pregnant again with my seventh child.

The last thing I need was another child by another man. I knew right away that I could not have this baby. I asked around to see how I could terminate the pregnancy.

Now, Jackson did not like the thought of us terminating the pregnancy, but I thought that he had agreed to give me the money and to also take me to the airport. The cost to terminate a pregnancy in those days were extremely expensive. At that time, there was no place in this region to have an abortion. I had to fly out to New York to have it done.

Jackson's mother was praying that I would not do it, as well as my aunt. I tried to explain to my aunt that I already have five kids to take care of. I had just got this good job at General Motors. This was a dream job. I was freshly back from a layoff and now I would need maternity leave. I was so afraid that they would fire me, and I needed this job to take care of my babies. I recall my aunt saying, "Lizzie, don't get rid of this child. This may be the very child that will take care of you when you are older and in need of some help."

The day that I was to go to New York, Jackson never showed up with his half of the money. Nor did he take me to the airport. I cried and called him a sorry so-and-so. I had no idea what God had in plan for me and this baby. All I knew was I could not afford to have this baby. I called Jackson's mother to see if she had seen him or knew his whereabouts. She answered the phone saying, "Thank God you're not gone. I was praying all night that you would not go through with it."

I had the baby! Right now, I am so glad that I had her. I can not imagine my what my life would be like without her. She has been a great help to me throughout her life.

Jackson promised that he would never leave me. He promised to always take care of me and his child. He was in our life for approximately five years before I really ended the association. While in the relationship, he cheated on me countless times. He was not able to commit to me and me only. He was great with the kids but not so great to me. Where he left his responsibility as a parent, his mom picked up the slack. She helped in many ways. All my kids called her grandma. Bit, her nickname, was a very gracious person. I appreciated all her acts of kindness.

I judged Jackson to be a good person because he helped me get my children. We faced so much trouble while trying to get them back home. I still appreciate him to this day because of that very reason. But I learned from him a lot of what to take and what not to take in a relationship.

Even now, I believe that everyone that has came into our lives are not meant to stay forever in our lives. Some were just meant to be a mere season in that time span. We need to recognize who is and who is not destined to be but for a short span of time. We can only be aware of the beginning and ending of a season through the Holy Spirit. I refer to the Holy Spirit often because John 14:26–27 lets me know that without the Helper, I can do nothing.

Obviously, I was so tired. I had no directional compass that I could benefit from. I only had calendar aids and reminders. I was the mother of seven children by three different fathers. My first child was out of wedlock. My next five children were by first husband. My next child came after my divorce. One by one. Five by one. One by one. Obviously, there are no further explanations required to explain how my actions were accomplished.

I was searching for love. I did not understand that my underling self-image was blurring my vision. It should have been obvious my choices in men were not up to par. It was not because I was a bad person. I was looking through a distorted reality. It should have been obvious, but it was not to me.

I KNOW THIS SOUNDS CRAZY

For a long period of time. I did not appreciate the simplest of attributes or the ability to discern the idea of attributes in the first place. I would downplay my God-given features. For example, I would dress down not bring attention to myself. I was afraid someone would think I was a "normal" human being. Normal human being in the sense that everything in my life was under control. I know that this sounds crazy. But deep down inside me, I felt I was not worthy of what was called a" normal life." Having everything under control was never a part of my reality. Feeling unworthy became my own mental plan of action. My thought process for my reasoning was that if anyone really knew this about me, they would not love me. I know that this sounds crazy. But I allowed my schemes to become a guest in my mind. I believed my mental issues of unworthiness schemes to be true.

The next few years of my life was a little more confusing. During those years, I had not realized that a lot of my pain I suffered were from these black holes that I had inside of me. They would never heal and anytime someone would touch them, I would cry out in pain. They really were sores that never healed...life's trauma and scares.

Now, at the age of thirty-four, I had accepted that this is what life had dealt me. I settled to just live with it because I had never had the pleasure of experiencing life otherwise. I would go on living life with my guard up, especially around my heart. I dared not to dream or imagine that my life could be anything different. I had a trust level that started and ended at zero. I refused to let anyone into my personal space. I always was suspicious of anyone and everyone. I trusted no one. I held on to the fact that my father was killed, and my mom left me on the steps. I had no feelings. I grew more numb by the day and I made sure that I never showed any emotions. I was doing things that I knew were out of character for me like hanging out drinking and trying to fit in or trying to date men I knew were not my type. I felt as if everyone saw me as I saw myself: a stupid, dumb misfit. I had nothing real to attach myself to. No immediate family. Just me against the world. I felt extremely unprotected. No one to fight for me. I remember wondering to myself, *what kind of a person do not have anyone*. So, I poured all my efforts into protecting my kids. I took pride in taking care of them no matter what. I always made sure that they were safe. I was not going to leave them like my parents did me.

It was hard raising them. I taught them the little that I knew. I showed them that they were loved. I also helped my kids to develop character because I knew character was the key for many opportunities that they would have in the future. I demanded that they stay out of trouble and that they treated others as they would like to be treated. I encouraged them to always be respectful and kind and to be honest and to wear integrity well. If you are able, help others that are in need. It was not much, but I engraved these things into their hearts.

I eventually met a gentleman. He was a little older than me, but he was a kind, self-sufficient man. His name was Toomer. He was about five-foot-nine, medium-brown complexion with a mustache. Chiseled muscles everywhere. Very neat, exceptionally clean and highly organized man. He had a smile that would brighten your day and was a self-assured and stable person. A little rough around the edges, but kindhearted on the inside. I remember meeting him at the factory where we worked at. I did not see him again for a long time. It had been about a year after meeting him in the factory that I saw him again at Kmart. He asked for my phone number. I told him he could look it up in the phone book. The name I gave him was a real name that I used to list my number under, but it was not my name. A week later he spotted me outside of a record store.

He yelled, "Aye girl, you gave me the wrong number. Wait right here, I be out in a few minutes."

I Know This Sounds Crazy

At the time, I was with one of my best friends. She was driving my car. We waited for a few minutes and proceeded to pull off when he came out of the record shop. I did not want him to know that I lived right down the street from the store. I told my best friend to drive to her house. He followed us there. He pulled up and asked what we were about to get into. We said nothing important. He asked if we wanted to have a drink and we said yes. He then told us to follow him to his house. After what seem like a long time, we came to a nice apartment complex across town from where I lived. We went in and he poured drinks and we listened to music that he had just brought at the record store.

I remember him telling me that he was from Muncie, Indiana. He had moved to Anderson to be closer to his job. As he shared his life's story with me that evening, I felt comfortable with him enough to share my life's story. We had a few things in common. We both experienced some hard times and we both had been emotionally, physically, and mentally hurt. He had seven kids and I had seven kids.

My best friend and I enjoyed our evening with Toomer. Before we left, I gave him my phone number. He called me the next day and we saw each other everyday from that point. We eventually became close. Toomer introduced me to his adult children. I introduced him to my babies. My oldest was sixteen and my baby was six. Toomer took an interest in my children. He planned movie nights at his house and he would pop popcorn for us all. Other weekends we would hang out with his kids as they came over to visit him.

Toomer and I were both searching for something. Mostly happiness. Toomer loved to cook. We would have dinners together. We spent the holidays cooking and hosting our family and friends. I loved Toomer because he was a confident and self-made man. I recall him saying things like, "I don't have to wait until Friday to take you out. I keep money and I can take you out any day of the week." For some reason, that statement impressed me. Toomer was not like my father; he made provision for his life by working hard, saving money, and paying his bills on time. He stayed and watched his kids graduate high school. He believed in quality, not quantity.

There were times that I wondered why and how we were working so well together. Didn't he see these flaws inside of me? I know he knew my story, the one I rehearsed often to disqualify myself fit to be loved. I had never seen the beauty in which God had created me.

BUT GOD SAVED ME

At the age of forty-one, I was tired. A school dropout. No mother. No father. Siblings that were scattered out there somewhere. I asked God, who am I and what on earth am I here for? I had gone to church to know and believe that there is a God. For some reason, I believed I was not His favorite person. I was not worthy due to the circumstances I was born into. I did not think that God wanted or liked me. I was a misfit. Back then, I was very naïve about the way God operates. As I reminiscence, I was naïve about life in general.

I had a great job. I had a car. A place to live. Seven beautiful children. A lot of associates but no real, pure love. There was a void in me that I could not figure out how to fill it. I tried alcohol. I tried men. I tried getting money. I tried hanging with my friends. I even tried to smoke a joint a few times because that is what my friends were doing to help with their issues in life. I tried to fit in, but to no avail. No matter what I did, nothing would or could fill the hunger for love and to be accepted.

There was a young lady that lived across the street from me. She had three babies of her own. She was a little younger than I. She kept herself very neat and clean. Through a few short conversations that we had, I learned that she was separated from her husband. We had similarities. We were single mothers trying our best to do right by our kids. There were many more thing we had in common, but I would not find out until one holiday.

It was one Thanksgiving in the mid-1980s. She came over to my house and asked if she could use my phone.

I said, "Yes, but why are you not celebrating Thanksgiving with your family?"

She explained that she had no family to celebrate with. She had been an orphan until she was five years old. She was adopted by this lovely lady that had just passed about time she told me her story. While she shared her story with me, all I thought about was *she is like me.* We both had no family. No mother and no father. She had experienced rejection and abandonment just like I had. After our conversation that Thanksgiving, we clicked and became friends, to best of friends, to family.

About a year after we started our friendship, she invited me to go to this church meeting. She had been to a service before. That very invitation was the beginning of the rest of my life. I decided that I would go with her.

It was an evangelist that I now know was sent by God. I absolutely believe that He sent her just for me. Her name was Marilyn Griffin. She was hosting church in the basement of a house that she was renting.

I remember that Sunday the evangelist called me up to the front where she was teaching.

She said, "Sweetheart, the Lord wants to save you. If you would give Him your heart, God would not only save you, but He will heal all the hurt and pain."

I said, "You don't know I drink and have a boyfriend."

She replied, "Do not worry about that. He will deliver you and set you free from things that have had you bound in the past, like witchcraft and poverty. He will save your house. And that special someone, your boyfriend, God said if you allow Him to save you, He will save him and give him back to you."

By this time, I was on the floor saying yes to God. That day something happened. It was all new to me, but it felt so good. Was this real? Something or someone had taken complete control. The best way I can describe it is that locked door was now opened. It was as if I was let out of some sort of a prison.

I was delivered from alcohol that day. God took the taste away from me. I broke up with my boyfriend, Toomer. With this newfound freedom, I had to find out who I was and what was I supposed to do now that I was free. To be born again, I needed to know what all of that meant.

But God Saved Me

I had been sitting on those steps for forty-one years. I was just like the man at the Pool of Bethesda. I was stuck there until Jesus came along and told me that I could get up off those steps.

My pain was so deep that I hurt from it every single day since the first incident happened. I could never be happy in life. My life was just always okay. I was still crying from the steps and no one ever heard me for forty-one years. Every bad thing that happened to me I thought I deserved it. Whenever I was taken advantage of, I would think I deserved it. It had been a pattern in my life. Most of the time I was mistreated by the very ones that was supposed to protect me.

It seemed as though I wore these signs that defined me by saying: *Here I am, you can beat me*. I wore the sign that said, *you can molest me*. I wore the sign that said, *you can lie on me*. I wore the sign that said, *you can steal from me*. I wore these signs. I had liberty but never understood how to walk in the grace of God. I was too busy wearing signs. I did not see myself how the Father saw me. It was an illusion of the enemy that I saw when I looked at my reflection. I believed the lies he showed me. While washed in the blood of the lamb, I saw the uncleanliness of my past. Oh yes, I wore the signs.

Often, times, we resort or surrender our strengths to randomness. Randomness, by trial and error. Living by randomness in the end often brings us bad news and unsatisfactory results. Many years, I fumbled through my life blindly. But God saved me.

I knew it was too late for a lot of things. I remember feeling safe now knowing God loved me. It was nice to feel like I belonged to someone. To know someone genuinely cared for me. I love Him for loving me. For me, it did not matter now if no one else loved me, just if God did. For the first time, I felt like I had a daddy. By me now possessing a dad, I was going to be okay. I was happy for once that I had did something right. I felt fulfilled. I needed absolutely nothing more to fill all those voids in my life. I tried many things, but nothing ever fit. But God!

I no longer felt alone. I was so elated. My new life was illuminating around me. Now when people would see me, they would say, "Liz, what happened to you. Look at you, you look different."

I would say, "It's Jesus. I found Jesus." Then for some reason, I would weep or smile. I had never been noticed like that before. Finally, I was seen how I always wanted to be seen. Then they would ask what made you try Him.

I would reply, "I had tried everything else, so, I thought why not try Jesus."

I stopped relying on people and I started relying on God. God became everything that I had been missing in my life. I began to encompass everything the Word of God said I could be and become. For the first time in my life, I felt Agape love. An unconditional love. He had become a mother and a father to me. He knew my past, my failures, my mistakes, my issues and yet He still loved me. Saw beyond all my flaws that in my opinion would have disqualified me to be loved properly. I was an orphaned abandoned by my mother, rejected by many, but God saved me on that Sunday thirty-four years ago. He also saved my boyfriend Toomer. We were married three years after that.

CUES AND SYMBOLS

Because so much of my past has been heavily influenced by rejection, abandonment, and voids, the stains remained reflecting my unworthiness. I learned to react to these cues and symbols from the pains and holes that mangled my heart and lingered on from my past.

Thus, I was again stuck on the steps. The holes inside my heart would not allow me to hold on to what God had done for me in my life. I kept reacting to the mental and emotional cues and symbols of a broken heart. I had trained myself to jump to conclusions from the experiences of my past cues and symbols.

Now that I am in Christ, I am a new creature; "old things are passed away; behold all things become new" (2 Cor. 5:17). I had to learn that it was a process in which I had to walk through, grow through, heal from, let go of, and be delivered from. The pain of my past had me stuck on them same steps as six-year-old me until now. While I would be listening to the Word of God and the enemy would say, "That is not for you. You're the exception to the rule. Things like that are not going to happen for you, after all you don't have a normal past. Too much has happened to you. You didn't graduate. You were abandoned by your mother. Your father died because he was a gambler."

Letting go of my past and pain was not as easy as I thought it would be. Every time I would try to deal with letting go, fear would come over me. I would be filled with anxiety. Many times when I would have to get up in front of people or talk to someone that was superior to me, tears would start to flow. I always felt like everyone could see right through me. They could see all the inadequacies. I believed the adversary when it came down to disqualifying me to take my rightful place in the kingdom of God.

A few times, I went to go see a psychologist. When the conversation stopped and it was quiet in the room, I felt as if the psychologist was staring at me, which made me feel uncomfortable. I would think to myself, *What is he looking at? What issue or flaw does he see in me?* I assume that he saw all my imperfections.

He would say, "If you want to know what I see, just ask me."

I said, "What do you see?"

He replied, "I just see you with a yellow shirt and black pants on. I only see the outer appearance. I am not a magician and I cannot see through you."

Now, I know that is what the enemy had done to me all those years. He had me feeling like everyone had x-ray vision and could see the imperfect me.

Months later, I was at the altar praying. I was asking God, "Why am I filed with fear?"

He quietly answered me by saying, "You do not truly believe that I really love you like I say in my Word."

Wow, here I was thinking that I am a faithful believer of the Word of God, but issues had me deceived.

"There is no fear in love, but perfect love casts out fear" (1 John 4:18 ESV).

By God telling me that I was not believing His Word to be true, I had to go check myself. Often people believe that God can and will do exactly what He said He will do for others, but not for themselves. I saw that I needed to go back in this race and learn to love what God loves, which is me. I must learn to love me.

I was tired of the excuses of being traumatized, abandoned, and rejected having control over me. The trauma from my life experience had me bound in a cycle of defeat. Trauma is a demonic attack. It has memories that play back anytime someone or something triggers a feeling that is associated with that incident.

In a Christian book I once read, the author reveals the reason why more people do not get their deliverance is the same door of pain they walked through, is the same door of pain they must walk back through it in ordered to be healed. Most of us never wants to relive the trauma, but it is necessary to be healed and delivered. If you chose to stay in that environment, it will destroy you.

"The thief comes only to steal and kill and destroy; I have come that they may have life and have it to the full" (John 10:10 NIV).

Frequently, we assume that it will just go away on its own, but it never does. That thing has taken up residency in our minds and body. Now it has become an issue of yours. Scripture tells us to guard our heart for out of it flows the issue of life (Prov. 4:23). We must learn how to ask God to show us ourselves. What issues or area do I need to be dealing with so I may obtain my healing? I prayed for God to heal me. One by one, He healed me as I surrendered unto His will.

One of my issues or insecurities was that I did not get my diploma. General Motors had a program that offered their employees an opportunity to get a GED while getting compensated for it. The classes were five days a week, for eight hours a day. We had to report to class as if it were our regular forty-hour-a-week job. After the classes had begun, several people dropped out and went back to work. I assume it was because they could not deal with the demand of an eight-hour school day. It was made known that if you did not go those eight hours you did not get paid.

I recognized that this opportunity was an open door for me. I signed up for the program. This leg of the race was not going to be easy for me. I am now forty-four years of age. Sometime ago I discovered that I have a learning disability. Once I realized what I had gotten myself into, fear and anxiety hit me. I began to struggle with my assignments.

God started talking to me about finishing school. Quitting was not an option for me. God would not let me stop mid-stream. This was a necessary for my healing process. It was essential for my journey in life.

The first time I took my test for my GED, I flunked. I allowed the fear to grip me and I developed test anxiety. I am not sure of how many points I needed to pass. I just remembered that I failed by thirteen points. I signed up for the next class. It is all new students in the class except for me. I was embarrassed. I felt as if everyone knew that I had failed. Here came those old familiar sprits telling me that I was not good enough. I was not smart enough. Your mother abandoned you and your father died. Rejection is your portion. Satan came with all his lies like he normally does. I did not give in to his devices.

I went back and attended all the classes a second time. When I took the test for the second time. I missed passing by six points. I had to humble myself and retake the class all over again. A third time. This was more than humbling. This was the Potter putting me back on the wheel.

I believe now that God was remolding me. He allowed me to learn how to endure and persevere for my future journey.

Now, that I was on my third attempt in taking this class, I had to rely on God to open up my mind to receive the information being taught. I had a nice instructor and he encouraged me to continue trying.

My husband would say, "Liz, anything worth having is worth fighting for." I was determined that I was going to get my GED. After I finished the class this time, I had to drive to the next town over to take the test. I sang praise songs on the trip over to the testing facility site. I had three subjects to be tested on. I thought if I get at least two points in all three subjects, I will have my six points need pass.

I brought my lunch so after each subject, I would take a break and snack on something. I finished the first test. I went out of the room to snack on the food that I had brought. When I looked up from my lunch bag, I saw the instructor that was administering the test walking toward me.

He stated, "Lizzie, that's it, you got all six points on your first subject. You passed!"

Cues and Symbols

I froze at first. Suddenly, I began to weep. At the age of forty-five, I had finally conquered an issue that has held me captive for years. I felt a burden lifted off me. I had a breakthrough.

I now know that "I can do all thing through Christ who strengthens me" (Phil. 4:13). Reading the Word of God and knowing and believing the Word of God are two different things. From that experience, I absolutely can believe the Word of God. I tried the Spirt and found it to be of God (John 4:4). For the first time in life I took one step down in order to attempt to get off those steps.

I associated with a group of like-faith people. We worked together for GM. We would often share testimonies, ideals, and information with one another that was greatly beneficial. One of the group members shared with us that we could go to Bible college and our job would pay us for it. Just hearing that information caused a fear to rise in me once again. I had barely gotten my GED. I assure you that I was not college material. Besides, I was now fifty-four years old. God was up to something, but I did not know that then.

At the church that I was a part of, we had a guest speaker come teach one Sunday. The lesson was about continuing or finishing the assignment God had purposed for you. During his teaching, he gave a word of acknowledgement.

He spoke, "Someone is contemplating going back to school, but you are worried about your age. You are thinking about when you graduate in three or four years, you will be too old. Let me ask you this: how old will you be in three or four years if you do not go back to school?"

With that statement, I knew I had to register for college. I was shaking in my boots, but I enrolled. I was scared and on many of the days I cried. I wanted to give up, but I felt the hand of God in the middle of my back pushing me to continue. I frequently thought, *this day will be my last day in college.*

The first year of college was almost over. Before we were to take our finals, the last assignment we had to do was to give a fifteen-minute message/sermon. We were to pray and ask God what topic we were to speak about. I heard a topic on *Women in Transition Homes*. Part of the assignment was for us to critique each other. Did they speak clearly? Did they stay focused on the topic? Did they speak in a timely fashion? I hated to be critiqued. It took me back to that little girl being deemed inadequate. Those old familiar thoughts tried to come back to haunt me. I got through the message. I was extremely relieved when I finished it.

On my way home, which was about a twenty-minute ride, the presence of the Lord was in my truck. I had never experienced this type of presence before. It was powerful. The Lord came and spoke to me on the drive home.

He stated, "Yes, I did choose you and I have called you."

I responded with, "God, what is this all about?"

God replied, "You never thought this could happen to you...you going to school. You are conquering your worst fears. Now you can go and tell someone what I have done for you. Let them know that I can do it for them as well."

Two days later, God dropped in my spirit a women's ministry.

I asked, "What would I call it?"

God said, "What do you want the women to know?"

I replied, "That they are not alone."

That was the moment Y.A.N.A. (You Are Not Alone) Ministries was birthed. I started off by having monthly cell meetings in my house. Then we start having meetings in a facility. Before I knew it, we were having conferences once or twice a year.

Knowing that I was truly hearing from God gave me a feeling of excitement. The challenging part is with hearing there comes having to be obedient. God was telling me to leave the church I was attending. I had not a clue to where He wanted me to go. It was a good church, but God wanted me to get more. More of what, I was not sure of. I had to be obedient. I obtained a Christian Workers license and an associate degree in theology.

I read somewhere that there are a few levels to hunger. One was starving; you will eat anything to be satisfied. Another one is hungry; you eat because you need to. The one that I was at was hungrier; I have eaten but I still desire more. I wanted and needed more of God.

I would be in a church service and feel all alone. I wondered why this was. I watched people come in with various issues and hurts. After the preacher preached his same ole' sweet by and by message, the people would walk right back out the church door with those same issues and hurts. I could not quite understand why the "Church" was not helping more people. That was a real concern for me. As God's servants, why weren't we doing more to meet the needs of the hurting? I knew what happened to people that go to church and do not get the help that is needed. What are we doing about the hurting and the downtrodden? I know that there is more to this lifestyle than just accepting what life has thrown at you.

As I managed to press forward in life, I learned that God always had my back. A lot of times it was not easy, but those that are led by the Spirit are the sons of God. God led me to another church. During that time, I had an opportunity to attend a ministry-equipping school in southern Indiana, approximately two hours away from my hometown. It is a sister school of Christian International Ministry Network in Santa Rosa Beach, Florida.

My first visit to this equipping school was mind-blowing. I thought, *is what I am seeing is true?* Is there such a ministry that really helps people to become all that God desires them to become, to be taught and trained to minister to the hungrier saints?

Not only does this school help you to identify your purpose in God, but it also trains you in those giftings. It taught me more about kingdom purpose, doing things God's way not the world's way, and how to flow in apostolic and the prophetic giftings. I felt like this school, this network, is my DNA. I fit in. Destiny had been calling and I answered the call.

REOPENED WOUNDS

I was living and loving myself better than I ever had. This was a season where I started to really believe and understand I am that woman God created me to be. Not only was I now standing on those steps I was left on, but I literally stepped down a few of those steps. This is a nice place to be.

One evening, I received a call from an unfamiliar person. It was a nephew from Florida. One of my sister's sons. Now I did not keep in contact with my siblings over the years, nor did they keep in contact with me all except for Bird, my sister in Cleveland. He stated that he had overheard conversation about an auntie he had in the state of Indiana that he never met. He was inquisitive about me and somehow found my number and called me. He introduced himself to me. We both was extremely excited to hear from each other. He informed me about a family reunion that was going to take place in Alabama that summer. This was my mother's side of the family. He gave me the information to call the person that was organizing the family reunion. By now my mother has passed from this life into eternal life. I was thinking I could still find out some information about my family.

My husband and I, my two daughters and two of my sons, along with three of my grandchildren went. I saw so many of my relatives that I was thrilled to meet. I began to feel connected to my roots. After all these years of being disconnected now, I was finally getting linked back up. This part of the healing process felt good. No, it felt great! I left that weekend feeling fulfilled and empowered.

It is now a year or two later and once again, my mother's side of the family was having another reunion. The first reunion had gone so well that I was excited to go to this one. I wondered what family members I would get to meet this time that I had not had the privilege to meet previously. We were to order T-shirts that had our family name starting with my grandmother Cora Lee and her offspring. My mother is the oldest of my grandmother's children. When it was time to receive the T-shirts, I noticed that everyone of my grandmother's children had a picture of them on the T-shirt except for my mother.

I asked the planning committee, "Where is my mother's picture?"

They stated that no one had or could find a picture of her. "We all looked."

The picture frame on the T-shirt where my mom face such have been was left blank.

I was devastated. I looked forward to seeing where I had come from, but there was nothing. An empty blank space. I thought this is how my whole life had been, *blank*. No connection to my mom and where I had come from. This situation angered me. I got mad with my mom all over again. I blamed her for disconnecting from her family and siblings. All my aunts had stayed in contact with each other except for my mom. They all had relationships with one another. They all went to the same church. Their kids all grew up together. My aunts and cousins seemed to be a close-knit family except for my mom and her kids.

Once again, I did not feel a part of or connected to my family. I did not get the chance to see where I had derived from. Where are the people who conceived me? No mother. No father. That blank space spoke volumes to me. It said you came from nowhere and no one.

That wound had been reopened. I thought that I had been healed from this type of rejection, not understanding that it is a process to healing. I read more books and scriptures on deliverance. I needed this to make sense to me. I needed to understand the pain that would come out of nowhere and choke me up. I read this book by a Christian author who came from a dysfunctional relationship with her mother. As I read this book I started to cry. I called a friend and asked her if could I just cry and vent to her. Being the good friend that she is, she said yes. Through this book, I began to understand generational curses. There are curses that are tied to a family's bloodline. I recognized that I had more work to do in order to be delivered and stay delivered. I had come too far to not be totally healed and to sustain my healing.

I began to thank God for my life.

In prayer one day, God spoke to me and said, "Daughter, you are mine. Your parents were just the vehicle I used to get you here. I know you. Before you were shaped in your mother's womb, I knew you. Before you saw the light of day, I had holy plans for you."

I finally got it. I realized whose I was. The voice was loud and clear. It was as if God was standing before me. He was correcting my thoughts and behavior like a good father who loves His child would do. This is part of the journey. To allow God to protect, lead, and keep me on the path He has set before me. I had to trust God to guide me. He knew where He wanted to take me. I had to believe and declare who God said I am. I allowed God to turn that *logos* word into *rhema* for me. It did not take long to regain my strength. I commanded my thoughts to be the thoughts that God has toward me. I am the child of a king. I must see myself how the Father sees me and that is *whole*. I learned to relax because He is in control of my destiny.

THE CALL OF LIFE: WHERE DESTINY MEET PURPOSE

Approximately two years after going to C.I. equipping school and MSG (Ministering Spiritual Gifts) School, my whole world changed. During those years I had gone through some valleys. When destiny is calling, you want to escape the test and trials, but He who has called you out of darkness into His marvelous light is with you.

"I am sure of this, that He who began a good work among you will bring it to completion by the day Jesus Christ" (Phil. 1:6). The work had already begun.

I found myself in a small remnant of believers that was left after the church we were attending closed. We felt as if God purposed for us to stay together. We had a few discussions about what we were going to do now. We prayed and asked God what direction we were to go. He led us to start gathering. Out of that remnant, it was about six or seven of us that were ministers. We need God's directions on how were to organize and operate. That led us to pray, fast, and seek the Lord for answers.

We started renting an unoccupied church building. The former owners of the building had just built a new Worship Center. We met on Wednesday for Bible study and on Sundays for worship. We would take turns teaching and ministering each week until we got clear instructions from the Lord. We were waiting on God to either raise someone in the group of ministers to shepherd or send us a shepherd. We were certain God would send us a solution.

One of the saints had a brother that was an apostle aligned with C.I. He lived in Columbus, Missouri, but visited his family in Anderson often. I inquired about when was he coming to visit and if he would be interested in meeting with us. I let him know that we are seeking the Lord for instructions. He agreed to seek the Lord on our behalf.

A few months later, he came to visit. We set up an informal meeting with a few of the ministers and saints at his sister's house on Friday night. On Saturday, we had a service that night. He let us know that he had heard from the Lord.

He spoke to us and said, "I have sought the Lord about this ministry. Yes, you are supposed to be a church." Then he looked at my husband and I and said, "You and your husband are to be the senior pastors."

I fell to the floor. I was in array of emotions. Later I asked my husband what his thoughts were about what was said.

Toomer said to me, "Liz, if God said it than that is what it is. I know in my spirit we are to do what the Lord said to do. I am certain you are to be the lead pastor, and I am to undergird you and co-pastor with you and together we are the senior pastors."

A few days later, I went over to my youngest child's house. When she answered the door, I told her that they just said that I was to be the pastor of this church. I was gripped with fear.

She looked at me and said, "Who else is supposed to be pastor, Mom? It has been prophesied that you were called to be a pastor." She said it so calmly and matter of fact.

I remember when my husband and I would go to visit different churches and the ushers at the door would always ask my husband if he is a pastor or minister so they could seat us in the minister section of the church. I know that it had been prophesied that were called to be a pastor, but for some reason, I did not comprehend it in its entirety. I thought Y.A.N.A. Ministries was the women's group I was to pastor. Toomer had a men's group that he mentored and labored with. I believed that they were flock of sheep he was to shepherd, not the whole church.

My husband was calm about it. That fear had me so tight that it caused me to be ill. Fear paralyzes your purpose and your destiny. Its intent is to eat up every desire God has placed in your heart. The scripture affirms that fear brings torment. I had learned and read enough about warfare prayers. I had to war over this spirit of fear. I realized that it was controlling me.

I studied scriptures about fear and what God reveals about how to handle it. I prayed faithfully concerning the spirit of fear. I meditated on these scriptures daily.

> Be anxious for nothing, but in everything by prayer and supplication, with thanksgiving, let your request be made known to God; and the peace of God, which surpasses all understanding, will guard your hearts and minds through Christ Jesus.
>
> Philippians 4:6–7

"I can do all things through Christ who strengthens me" (Phil. 4:13).

"Therefore, if anyone is in Christ, he is a new creation; old things have passed away; behold, all things have become new" (2 Cor. 5:17).

"For you did not receive the spirit of bondage again to fear, but you received the Spirit of adoption by whom we cry out, 'Abba, Father'" (Rom. 8:15).

"For God has not given us a spirit of fear, but of power and of love and of a sound mind" (2 Tim. 1:7). This was my regiment. I had to war for my deliverance.

> For the word of God is living and powerful, and sharper than any two-edge sword, piecing even to the division of soul and spirit, and of joints and marrow, and is a discerner of the thoughts and intents of the heart.
>
> Hebrews 4:12

I had to put the word of God on that spirit until my deliverance came. Now, sometimes that spirit comes to see if the Holy Spirit is still occupying his old home. I have a sign on my heart that says, "Fear, there are no vacancies here!" I am no longer paralyzed by it. I am free to be who and what God has called me to be.

"Before I formed you in the womb, I knew you; Before you were born, I sanctified you; I ordained you a prophet to the nations" (Jer. 1:5).

He knew my frailties, insecurities, and fears. Yet, he ordained me to be a vessel of honor. To partner with Him to get people delivered and set free. He gave me the keys to the kingdom. The power to bind whatever is not of Him. To loosen whatever He had already loosened.

I submitted to the will of God. We started pastoring. We all decided to call the church New Covenant Ministries for we, the remnant, had a new covenant with our heavenly Father. He started to grow the church as we followed God's instructions.

We moved and rented out another church for about three years. We were seeking the Lord for a building of our own. We fasted and prayed as a church concerning this. We found a church that was for sale. As a church, we went and visited the property. We were excited about the building. We put in our offer. The bank denied us. We were very confused because we knew that our finances were in order. As a matter of fact, the banks said our finances were impeccable. They denied us because they said we did not have a plan in place for future revenues.

Wow, that was an eye opener for us. We connected with an organization that helps churches to grow. We started to implement the agenda that was setup with this organization. In the meantime, we were still fasting and praying and awaiting God to give us our next set of instructions.

In the meantime, I had a friend that was in the banking industry. She called me to inform me that she had a client that said they was interested in selling their church. She gave me the information to contact them. As a church, we went and looked at the church. Everyone fell in love with it.

A few of the members from the selling church came to visit our church. I believe it was to see what kind of a people were interested in the church that they so loved. This group of saints had built this church in the 1970s. Now many of their members were up in age. A few members had passed away. They stated that they did not have youth that could take over the church.

While we were waiting to hear from God, my husband had a dream. In the dream, an angel visited my husband. He said there was a bright white light and the angel handed him the keys. Now, my husband does not say much in church but when he did, it was like E. F. Hutton talking. Everyone needed to listen. After that announcement, the whole church thanked, praised, and worshiped the Lord. A few weeks later, I woke up from my sleep. My television was on a Christian channel.

I heard this voice from the television say, "You need to write this down. God say you are approved."

I knew that word was speaking to me. I informed the church and once again we started thanking, praising, and worshipping the Lord. Not long after that, we got the call that we were approved to get the church.

It amazes me to this day what God did for us. The building that he blessed us with was three times larger than the building we were denied. It sits on ten acres. They left the building fully equipped with more than we could ever need. They only took personal property with them when they left.

God had done it again. I am in awe of Him. He never fails. He always causes His people to be triumphant.

PITFALLS; I NEVER SAW THEM COMING

I was secure in who I was in Christ. I was happy. I had married the love of my life. He adored me and I, he. We went on vacations and cruises. I was living the life that I thought I could. All my kids were grown and living their lives. Finally, all the holes in my heart were filled.

A few years ago, my third child fell on some difficult times. He was diagnosed with Type 2 diabetes. He moved in with my husband and me. We were happy to have him there. We both have gotten older and need his help. He helped with my husband. He would say, "Hey Toomer, let us get out of here and go for a ride. Let us leave these women here and go do man stuff. Do you want to go to Walmart?" By now we had found out that my husband had Parkinson's disease. My husband loved to go to Walmart.

My son was an incredibly special person. He was the one that did not get kidnapped by his father. He was the life of the party. He was the glue that helped his brothers to have a good relationship with each other. He encouraged any and everyone. I prayed often for him because he would stop on the highway or in a dark alley or in a snowstorm to help people who were in need. He was a gatekeeper in the church. He assisted the elderly, women, and children into the church. I recall seeing him run out to the cars and get people's Bible. If it were raining, he would be at their car door with an umbrella. If it were snowing, he would assist them in the church so they would not fall.

One day, about the end of August 2017, my son had been to the doctor for a follow-up appointment. The test results showed that he was low in potassium. It was a Thursday, and they were trying to find a place for him to get a potassium IV. They sent him to a hospital in another city. It was about thirty-five minutes from where we lived. This was set to take place in a two-day section. He went the first day and he came home, and things was fine. The next day, which was a Sunday, he came home from getting the potassium IV. He ate dinner and laid down. Approximately two hours later, he woke up in a lot of pain. I asked if he needed to go to the hospital, and he said yes. My husband, daughter, and I were on our way to go get some ice cream. We made our way to the emergency room. I dropped him off at the ER. My daughter took my husband and I back home. I know that my husband was not able to sit that long in the hospital while they were running tests on my son. Baby girl went back to the ER to sit with her brother..

I received the call from my daughter, and she said that they were sending her brother to Indianapolis. I asked for what? She let me know that his oxygen levels were dropping. They wanted to put him in ICU, but did not have any beds for him in that hospital. So, they called an ambulance to transport him to their sister hospital.

The next morning, he called to tell me that he would be okay, but they were keeping him for a few days. He said there was no need to come down and visit. A few days later, he called to say that the doctor wanted to intubate him to speed up the healing process. I went to see him before they were to incubate him but when I got there, they had already sedated and incubated him. I never heard my son's voice again. About two-and-a-half weeks later, we had to take him off life support. He had multiple organ failures. His kids, siblings, best friend, and I were there to say goodbye. It was one of the hardest situations we had to deal with.

We all gathered around his bed as his soul left us to be with the Father. All I could say to my family was, "I am sorry. I am so so sorry!" It was devastating to us all. I cannot explain or describe the hurt and pain. As I walked the hallway of the hospital, I wanted to continue walking right out the front doors and right into on coming traffic. Thank God for family and friends. They all consoled me as they grieved themselves.

I thought, *why would God allow this to happen? I been through a lot in my lifetime but this grief I could not handle. I cannot take this agony so You might as well take me now.* I was weeping from a fresh wound. I would rather for it to have been me instead. I had never utterly understood grieving. At that moment, there were no prayer or words that could have soothed my pain. I had no clue that you do not heal, you just adjust to the loss.

I watched my husband mourn and become saddened over our loss. There was a huge void in the house. As I stated before, he was an enormous help to us. I remember us talking about who was going to step up to help us with our daily needs. Toomer's older child was already helping us with his care but his third son said, "I got you! I will do so." And he did just that. This particular son had moved back from out of state a few years ago to be closer to his father and siblings.

I must say our children were a great support team for us. Our kids and some grandkids rallied around us and would not let us go without our needs and wants being met. They took turns coming to visit us and calling us to see if we needed anything. They would come and get my husband for the weekend to spend time with him. When I had to go out of town for ministry or family business, I never had to worry about him. His sons would say, "We got Pops. Go take care of business." I am grateful for their support. His son that moved back home would always tell me, "Do not thank me, this is my Pops. You do not have to thank me for what I am supposed to do."

Two years after my son passed, my husband's health started to decline more. I was not through grieving my son before I started to grieve the declination of my husband's health. He had been diagnosed ten years ago. He told me that he was tired and wore out from fighting this disorder. I knew what that meant. He was ready to rest.

We began to appreciate our life and what time we had left together. It was a sorrowful and joyous time. I made sure he knew how much I appreciated him. I do not know what or where I be in my life if God had not sent you to me. You are the best husband for me. I am the woman I am today because of your love for me. You gave me a since of identity. I knew who I was in the spirit because of God. In the natural, I know who I am because of you. I am who you are. We are one. We hugged and cried. We would continue to show our affection for one another.

I watched as our family started to feel that hurt that come from knowing their dad and stepdad would be leaving us soon. I watch our children trying to be strong for me all the while suffering internally. He has such a great impact on us all. My husband was an impactful man, father, and friend.

In December of 2019, right after the holiday, Toomer told me that he was ready to go.

"I am tired. I have no more strength to fight. Liz, you will be all right because Lola (his oldest daughter) will take care of you." I wept for I knew he was tired. I was not ready for him to go, but he was ready to rest in peace.

For the next two weeks, family friends and church family came to see him. Many prayed for his transition. I watched friends that he had mentored and loved unconditionally weep for my husband. They would tell me how much he meant to them. How his love for them changed their lives.

It was now a week into January 2020. The second Wednesday of the year. My youngest daughter, who had been living with us to help with our day-to-day living, had stayed up all night checking on Toomer. I would wake up often and check on him myself. Around 6:45 a.m., I looked in on my husband. He was still here with us. About an hour later, I heard him coughing. I said a prayer and tried to rest, but I could not. Approximately forty-five minutes after that, I went to check on him and he was gone.

I went to my daughter's room and knocked while saying, "Tiffany, he is gone. Your dad is gone."

I walked back into his room and felt his body. He was still warm. We called in the family. They came right away. The house was eerily silent but full of anguish and grief. I observed the discomfort in our family. The patriarch of the family was no longer with us physically. I had no words to console their hurt. I had no words to console myself. This time, I felt this aching deep within my heart. The love of my life was no longer here on earth.

It has been fifteen months since my husband's passing. I started writing this book just before my husband said he was ready to be with the Lord. It has been a long adjustment to his absence, all the while faced with this pandemic. With God's grace, I am getting through this. I lean on and depend on God. He knows me best. He has been there through every situation of my life. The Holy Spirit has been my comfort and strength.

THE SUM OF IT ALL

I realize that throughout my life, God was with me.

"Before I even formed you in your mother's womb, I know all about you. Before you drew your first breath, I had already chosen you" (Jer. 1:5a VOICE).

" For I know the plans I have for you, says the Eternal, "plans for peace, not evil, to give you a future and hope-never forget that" (Jer. 29:11 VOICE).

God knew of all my failures, insecurities, and fears, yet He ordained me to be a vessel of honor for Him. I was to partner with God to get His people delivered and set free.

I once believed that I was put here just so that people could beat me down. I once believed that I was a stem of weakness. A wilted stem with petals dying in fear and shame. Shameful of what I had came out of and fearful of the unknown. It took me many years to realize that God had given me the keys to the kingdom. I was endowed with power to bind whatever is not of God. To loosen whatever He desired or needed to be loosened.

When I look back over my life, I can see how the Lord led and guided me. God patrolled me from becoming devoured into the dust of the day and night. He patrolled me so that I became activated within Him with joy and delight. I learned how to embrace all that God was doing in my life. I learned how to accept the plans and path He has given me to walk. After all He is the Potter, and I am the clay. God's mercies are truly renewed every morning.

I can only advise you, but the Lord can change you. Anyone can give an opinion, but the details of your life will always come down to making the right decisions. There are many choices in life that might appear to be correct but only God can change your mindset and set you on the right path. You must allow Him to come into your life and make the necessary changes needed for you to become a conqueror.

I surrendered and yielded to His will and His way. I am still submitting to God every day.

It makes it much easier on me when I do not have to be in control. I do not care to be the driver when I have no clue to where I am going. So, I just move over and let Jesus take the wheel.

I thrive in His peace because I rest in Him. I started at the bottom of those steps but God has elevated me one step at a time until I was completely off the steps. The steps of a good man are ordered by the Lord. I am listening for directions as to where I am to step next. I am no longer that little girl that is in exile, but I am a woman who now walks in freedom.

CPSIA information can be obtained
at www.ICGtesting.com
Printed in the USA
BVHW080219091021
618423BV00007B/189

9 781637 694145